How to Be a Better Writer

by Elizabeth A. Ryan

Troll Associates

Library of Congress Cataloging-in-Publication Data

Ryan, Elizabeth A. (Elizabeth Anne), (date)
   How to be a better writer / by Elizabeth A. Ryan.
      p.   cm.—(Student survival power)
   Summary: Provides instruction on the practical parts of writing,
including how to make an outline, how to write a solid paragraph,
and how to finish up with a strong conclusion.
   ISBN 0-8167-2462-8 (lib. bdg.)   ISBN 0-8167-2463-6 (pbk.)
   1. English language—Composition and exercises—Study and teaching
(Elementary)—Juvenile literature.   [1. English language—
Composition and exercises—Juvenile literature.]   I. Title.
II. Series.
LB1576.R93   1992
372.6'23—dc20   91-3135

Contents

Introduction:
Feeling Confident About Your Writing

The first thing to remember about writing is this: *Everyone can write.*

That's right—everyone. There may be such a thing as a "born writer" (although even "born writers" have days when they think they'll never write again!), but there's no such thing as a "born not-writer." If you can read these words, you can write. At the very least, you'll be able to complete school assignments for compositions, book reports, and term papers. At best, you might even find yourself writing essays, journal entries, stories, poems, and articles for the school paper—for pleasure.

How is it possible to state so definitely that anyone can write? It's simple. Writing is something you learn—just the way you learned to talk. Think of the little children you know who haven't learned to talk yet. They have to cry, or wave their arms, or point to get what they want. Then, as they get older, they learn about words, and what a good job words can do. They learn not just to cry, but to say, "I'm hungry," not just to point, but to say, "I want that banana over there, and I want you to spread some peanut butter on it and bring it to me with a glass of chocolate milk."

You've learned this—and a lot of other things as well. Now you can use words to express your thoughts and feelings. You can say, "I don't think it's right to give homework over the weekend," or "I wish Terry and I were going to the dance together." As a person who knows how to talk, you can express a lot of complicated ideas in words. All it takes is practice.

If anyone can learn to write, then why do many people find it so difficult and scary? That's a tough question. Almost everyone, even people who have become famous writers and who have been writing for years, finds something difficult about writing. Maybe writing seems harder than talking because it's more permanent. You write something down and it's *there.* Sometimes it can seem as if the whole world is reading it and wondering why you wrote something so ridiculous! Many writers get around this problem by writing more than one draft. (In fact, writing several drafts is a good idea anyway, as we'll see later.)

Writing more than one draft means that you can remind yourself that *no one* will ever see your early writing. It's for you alone, just to figure out your ideas. Other writers start out by "brainstorming"— just making notes of whatever comes into their minds. This often feels more "private" and therefore easier than starting right out with "real" sentences. Some writers also pretend that they are writing only for the eyes of their closest friends—people who will love and appreciate them no matter what they write! As you can see, there are lots of different ways to get around feeling nervous about your writing.

Many writers feel as though there is a little critic—"Dudley Doolittle"—sitting on their shoulder, telling them to give up before they start. If Dudley is giving you a hard time, you may find it very difficult to get up the courage to pick up your pen and say what you have to say. This book will help you with a lot of the practical parts of writing. However, you have to get rid of Dudley Doolittle first! If you've decided before starting that you're not a good writer or that you don't have anything worthwhile to say, you're going to find it very difficult to write. You won't be able to think about what you want to write at all. You'll be too busy worrying about how bad it might be!

Remember, *you are an interesting person and you have something important to say.* Think of something you've done that you are proud of. Remember how interested your best friend was to hear you tell about something you did. Remind yourself of all the times that you've thought you were right in an argument or a discussion. Picture someone who would just love to know what you think about the topic you're writing about. If it helps, invent someone exactly like you—charming, witty, intelligent, good-looking... and modest! Find whatever way you can to remind yourself that your ideas are important, and you are going to share those important ideas by writing them down.

This book will help you with all the practical parts of writing—making an outline, writing a solid paragraph, and finishing up with a strong conclusion. Also, you will find that breaking the writing process down into several steps will help you to feel confident about your writing. If you only have to worry about one thing—*this* sentence or *this* paragraph—instead of the entire writing project and what everyone will think of it, you can concentrate all your energy. Worrying about the entire writing project can turn you into a Nervous Nellie or Hesitant Horace who doesn't want to write at all!

So get rid of Dudley Doolittle and take the writing process a step at a time. You just might surprise yourself by having fun!

Chapter 1:
The Writing Process
(What's It All About?)

While writing a composition, you go through many small steps. These small steps fit into five big categories: brainstorming, organizing, writing a first draft, revising, and editing. In this chapter, you'll get an overview of these steps. Later chapters will cover each category in more detail, breaking it down into smaller and smaller steps. Once you've gotten the "big picture" from this chapter, you can let yourself temporarily forget it in order to concentrate on one small step at a time. The smaller the step you are concentrating on, the easier it will be for you to give it your full attention before going on to give full attention to the next small step.

Brainstorming

Brainstorming means letting it all hang out—letting your thoughts run free in order to generate ideas. There are several different ways of brainstorming. But they all focus on one point: Forget about whether your ideas are good or bad, right or wrong—just keep them flowing. If you begin your writing activities by getting rid of critical Dudley Doolittle, the next logical step is to see what your mind can come up with when you have permission to think anything you want.

Many people who find writing difficult say that their trouble lies in "not knowing what to say." Often you may *feel* as though you don't have anything to say when, in reality, you are keeping back perfectly good ideas for fear of being wrong. Brainstorming gives you a chance to get your ideas out on paper. *Then* you can decide which will work and which won't.

Some people prefer to brainstorm from their original topics. If they were writing an essay on their interest in space travel, for instance, they might begin by listing the following ideas. Notice how the ideas are not in any particular order. They are not even written in full sentences.

Space Travel

could be fun	long time away from home
dogs in space	speed of light—go back in time?
rocket fuel	discover new planets
constellations	Saturn's rings—made of what?

The writer could then use these ideas to come up with a topic that is more focused than just "space travel," or to discover which parts of space travel the essay could cover.

Other people prefer to brainstorm in *clusters*. They think of different parts of a topic and then try to brainstorm on each one. This has the advantage of helping you organize your ideas before you start, but it may have the disadvantage of keeping your mind from feeling as free as you would like.

Here is an example of how someone might brainstorm in clusters about space travel.

Space Travel

Astronauts	Rocket Fuel	Discoveries
John Glenn	for long distances	new planets
training	stored where?	new stars
dangerous job		constellations
		Saturn's rings

Brainstorming is the time to think of ideas, not to criticize yourself. For more about brainstorming, see Chapter 3.

Organizing

Once you have a list of ideas, you'll need to organize them. To organize something is to put it in an order that makes sense—in other words, get it together! There are many ways of organizing ideas. The most important thing to remember is to choose a way that makes sense to you and will help your ideas make sense to your reader.

The organizing step is very important because it means that you don't have to write and put your ideas in order at the same time. An outline, a list of ideas, or some other form of organization that you prepare *before* you write means that you've cut your work in half. Thus, while you are organizing your ideas, you don't have to worry about *writing*—you can just concentrate on thinking.

Some school papers require research. You will have to go to the library to look up facts or to read one or more books or articles in magazines or newspapers. Book reports also require you to read a book. In those cases, you will have to organize your research, or the notes you made while reading the book.

One of the most useful forms of organization is an outline. An outline shows you the main ideas in your essay, but is often not written in full sentences. An outline for an essay on the history of space travel, for example, might look something like this:

History of Space Travel

I. Early space travel—only a dream
   A. Jules Verne—*Voyage to Another Planet*
   B. Ray Bradbury, science fiction of today
II. First flights
   A. *Sputnik*—1957, began Space Age
   B. *Explorer I*—1959, first U.S. satellite
   C. Yuri Gagarin—1961, first ship to go in orbit with a person on board
III. Big achievements
   A. *Apollo 11*, 1969—First people on moon!
   B. *Voyager* flights to Jupiter and Saturn

You can see how a writer would find it much easier to sit down and write an essay with this outline than to face a blank sheet of paper. Some outlines have even more detail, so that every paragraph has been mentioned in the outline before it is written. For more about organizing your ideas, see Chapter 4.

Writing a First Draft

As we've already discussed, the important thing to remember about the writing process is to take it one step at a time. After you've generated ideas by brainstorming and organized your ideas, perhaps into an outline, you're ready to start writing. Even then, however, don't look ahead to a polished final draft. Begin by ''roughing it''—by writing a first draft. This is a rough version of your essay that you will fix up later.

First drafts don't need to be spelled correctly or written in what is considered Standard English. They don't need to be perfectly worked out or beautifully organized. They only need to be written. Knowing that you will have a chance to fix up your writing later, you will find it much easier to get your thoughts down on paper. That's the purpose of a first draft. It allows you to get your thoughts on paper where they *can* be worked on later. For more about writing your first draft, see Chapter 5.

Revising

Once a first draft is written, you can begin to revise it. Read it over to see if you want to change any of your ideas and if the ideas you like are expressed clearly. Likewise, you can make sure that your ''tone of voice'' sounds the way you want it. Did you sound too serious when you meant to be funny? Did you use too many casual words when you were trying to write about something important? Finally, you can make sure that you have written an interesting opening and a strong conclusion.

As you can see, revising an essay means taking another look—writing at least one more draft after the first one. Some writers write several drafts, putting each one aside and coming back to it later to see if it sounds right. How many drafts you want to write will depend on you—both on your work process and on how important an essay is to you. In any case, however, you should be prepared to write at least one more draft after the first one, just to give yourself a chance to do your best work. Chapters 6-9 will help you revise your writing.

Editing

Once you have gotten your ideas into the shape that will best communicate to your reader, you are ready to *edit* your essay. First, make sure that you have corrected any mistakes in grammar and usage: no run-ons, no fragments, no dangling participles, and so forth. Then, *proofread* your essay to make sure that all words are spelled correctly and that your essay is correctly punctuated.

Some writers find themselves editing and proofreading their essays from the very first moment they sit down to write. They just don't feel comfortable doing it otherwise. If you are that type of writer, you will find a way to combine editing and proofreading with the other steps in the writing process. However, if you find that worrying about spelling and grammar is making you nervous or keeping you from getting the big picture of what your essay sounds like, you might try holding these steps for the end. Most of us find it a big relief not to worry about spelling and grammar until the very end. If you have been having trouble getting your ideas to come out as easily as you would like, save the editing and proofreading until later. You'll be surprised at how much more easily you write!

For more about editing, see Chapter 10; for more about proofreading, see Chapter 11.

Chapter 2:
Picking a Topic
(What Do You Write About?)

Getting Your Assignment Straight

Some writing assignments require you to write on a specific topic: Five hundred words on "Should the Driving Age Be Lowered?" or a ten-page paper on the natural resources of Bali. Some writing assignments give you a general topic that you are expected to make more specific. For example, you may be told to write something about your family, but it's up to you to decide whether it should be a family history, a collection of funny stories about your favorite aunt, or an explanation of what you'd most like to change about your family and why. Finally, some assignments are very open-ended. You may be told how many pages to write and when to turn them in, but everything else is up to you.

Whichever kind of assignment you've been given, the first thing to do is to *get it straight*. Nothing is worse than sitting down to work on an assignment and finding that you're not quite sure just what your teacher expects. Not only does it spoil a lot of writing time with worry, but there's also a very good chance that you could easily have fulfilled the assignment if only you had known what it was!

Here is a checklist of questions that you should be able to answer about any writing assignment. Some teachers make your life easier by spelling out the answers to each one of these questions when they give the assignment. Others expect you to know the answers, or assume you will ask. *Never be afraid to ask for more information about an assignment.* The more details you can get in class, the clearer the assignment will be for you and your classmates. If you're not comfortable asking questions in public, talk to your teacher in private. Either way, you'll avoid being unsure about what your teacher wants or finding out too late that you've guessed wrong.

Writing Assignment Checklist

____ Is there an assigned topic? If so, what is it?

____ If you are picking your own topic, does your teacher have to approve it? Is there a deadline for this? (Even if your teacher doesn't require it, it's often a good idea to clear a topic with your teacher first. Again, better safe than sorry!)

____ Are you expected to do research for this assignment? If so, how much? (It never hurts to check with a teacher about this question either, so that you know whether *research* means reading one article in the encyclopedia or really using the library. You can tell your teacher how many books or articles you've read and ask if they sound like enough.)

____ Does your teacher expect you to submit an outline or first draft? Are there deadlines for these steps? (In this book, we stress that you should not worry about spelling, grammar, or punctuation in either an outline or first draft—these are steps for *you*, not for a reader. If your teacher wants you to hand in these steps as well, find out if you are expected to write them in a form different from what you would write for yourself.)

_____ How long is the essay supposed to be?

_____ Does it have to be typed? (If so, make sure to double-space it and type on only one side of the paper!)

_____ If the essay can be handwritten, what are the rules for spacing, paper, color of ink, and so forth? (In general, it's best to use black or blue ink, skip every other line, and write on only one side of the paper, using wide margins. This makes it easier for your teacher to read and write comments on your work. Write neatly so that anyone can read your work easily. If you can't write neatly, get it typed. Remember, no one wants to read ''chicken scratch,'' writing that is very hard to make out. The harder you make it for your teacher, the harder he or she will be on what you write. Give yourself and your teacher a break.)

_____ When is it due? (Help yourself by writing the day of the week as well as the date. Nothing is worse than finding out on Tuesday that your paper is due on Wednesday!)

Getting Started

Whether you are given guidelines for picking a topic or are allowed to choose your own, you will find that it helps to develop a *writing purpose* and to keep that purpose in mind throughout the whole writing process.

A writing purpose is just what it sounds like—your reason for writing the essay or book report that you've been assigned. Of course, you may feel that your only purpose in writing is to get a passing grade! Nevertheless, you've probably already discovered that such a purpose isn't much help in motivating you when it comes to facing that blank page.

A better way to begin—no matter how you feel about grades and assignments—is to find a reason why it is important to you to explore and share your thoughts and feelings on the topic of your essay. Of course, it helps to pick a topic that you care about—and we'll discuss that later. Whatever your topic, you will find it helpful to imagine an *audience* and a reason why your audience *needs to hear* what you have to say on this topic.

To see how this works, let's say that you have been given one of the dullest topics ever in the history of writing assignments: You have been assigned, in November, to write two pages on "How I Spent My Summer Vacation." By this time, you don't really care how you spent your summer vacation, and you can't imagine that anyone else would either. Still, that's the assignment, and to get a passing grade, you've got to do it.

What will make it not only possible but perhaps also fun to complete this assignment is to find a reason of your own for writing it. What reason could you have for writing about your summer vacation?

A writing purpose always begins with an audience. Your reason to write is that someone needs to hear what you have to say.

So if you must write about your summer vacation, think of someone who would love to hear about it. If you can think of a real person, such as a distant relative or a friend in another city who didn't hear about your summer firsthand, so much the better. You can picture this person while you write, which should help you find something interesting to say. After all, if it interests your friend, then it must be interesting!

What if you can't think of a real person who wants to read two pages about your summer vacation? Use your imagination. Perhaps your audience is *you* five years from now. Think of where you hope to be in five years. Would that person find it interesting to remember last summer's vacation? Perhaps you can imagine someone in another country or from another planet who would like to know how Americans, or earthlings, or the people in your school spend their summer vacations. Maybe you can imagine someone who is simply fascinated by every little thing about you or who admires everything you do—would that person want to read this essay? If you can find some-one whom you *want to tell* about the essay topic, you're halfway home. Once you want to tell some-thing, you'll find you have the energy to write about it.

Narrowing a Topic

Many writing assignments are quite general. It may be your responsibility to make an assignment more specific. For example, if you are asked to write something about animals for a science class, that leaves you quite a bit of choice. What would your next step be?

What you are aiming for is to find a topic that is the right size for the length of the assignment. A ten-page assignment might be narrowed down to animals that humans have found useful in their daily lives.

Your next step, then, is to take the broad topic you were assigned and figure out a way to narrow it. Use your own interests to guide you. You might write down the first one or two or even five topics that come to mind when you hear the general topic, just to see where your thoughts are:

Assigned Topic: Animals

Your ideas:
  Animal Intelligence
  Pets
  Farm Animals
  Unusual Animals

Then ask yourself which topic seems most interesting to you. Let's say you choose "Animal Intelligence." This topic is still very broad. So think again of which ideas come to mind that will help you narrow the topic.

Topic: Animal Intelligence

Narrower topics:
  How Mice Are Trained to Run Mazes
  Are Cats More Intelligent Than Dogs?
  How Horses Are Trained To Run Races
  Whales and Porpoises—Some Very
    Intelligent Animals
  Chimpanzees That Learned to "Talk"

You can see how much easier it will be to find specific information on the narrower topics. You can make a general statement, give some examples, and come to a conclusion. The broader topics are so broad that you could say almost anything; it would be difficult to know when you had said enough.

Some people like to make upside-down "pyramids" to help them narrow topics. These pyramids get narrower and narrower, ending in a "point," or focused topic. Here are some examples of upside-down pyramids that might help writers narrow their topics:

Citizenship	*Stars and Constellations*
Responsibilities of a citizen	How the stars and
What you have to do to	constellations got
become a citizen of	their names
the U.S.	The story
	of Orion

Finding a Topic

Perhaps you have been given a very open-ended writing assignment, in which your teacher tells you the number of pages and the due date, but expects you to pick a topic of your own. Perhaps you have the option of finding your own topic and would like to give it a try, but aren't quite sure where to begin.

Whenever you pick your own topic, find something that interests you and that you care about.

It helps to choose something that you have strong feelings or ideas about. The more strongly you feel about a subject, the easier it will be to write about.

Here are some general categories of ideas that you might find you have strong feelings about, along with some specific suggestions for narrowing a topic to manageable size.

My Family
- ► My favorite/least favorite person in my family
- ► The funniest/saddest/best/worst thing that ever happened in my family
- ► What I love most about my family
- ► What I would most like to change about my family
- ► My family history

School
- ► If I were in charge of school...
- ► What our school really needs is...
- ► What I will miss most when I leave school
- ► The funniest/saddest/best/worst thing that ever happened to me in school
- ► What my ideal school would be like
- ► Schools in other countries (to narrow a topic, you would have to pick a specific country)

Television or Movies
- ► My favorite/least favorite movie or television program, and why
- ► My favorite/least favorite actor, and why
- ► Television makes me mad because...
- ► A funny/sad experience I had at the movies
- ► If I were a director/writer/actor, a television program or movie I would like to make would be...

► What I think is unrealistic about television or movies
► What I have learned from television or movies

Sports
► What it feels like to play my favorite sport
► What it feels like to watch my favorite sport
► An imaginary sport—what its rules are and how people feel about it
► The sports figure I most admire, and why
► If I were in charge of sports at this school...
► What it would feel like to be a star of my favorite sport
► A day in the life of a star of my favorite sport
► A history of my favorite sport in the United States
► A biography of the sports figure I most admire
► Sports medicine: what a sports doctor has to know
► A history of the Olympics
► The story of a sport that is played in other countries but seldom or never in the United States

Music
► What it feels like to listen to my favorite kind of music
► If I were a famous musician...
► A day in the life of a famous musician
► The musician or singer I most admire, and why
► The history of my favorite rock group
► The history of a musical instrument (to narrow the topic, you would have to pick a particular instrument, such as the guitar or the flute)

As you can see, you might have to narrow some of these topics still further, depending on the assignment. You can probably come up with even more ideas for each category listed here, as well as several other categories that interest you. Just ask yourself what you feel strongly about or have strong opinions about. Your own thoughts and feelings are your best guide.

Turning a Topic into a Thesis

So far, we've been talking about *topics*—ideas that you will write about. However, in order to guide you through your essay, you will find it helpful to have a *thesis* as well.

A thesis is a kind of an argument. It tells what you are trying to communicate to your audience. It is a way of expressing your writing purpose— what you want your audience to feel or think when they have finished reading your essay.

For example, "Whales and Porpoises—Some Very Intelligent Animals" could make a good topic for an essay. You would probably have to do some research; then you could state your main idea, give a few examples, and repeat your main idea to keep it strongly in your audience's mind. "Whales and Porpoises—Some Very Intelligent Animals" is your *topic*, but your main idea *about* the intelligence of whales and porpoises would be your *thesis*.

Thus, for example, your thesis might be "Whales and porpoises are far more intelligent than you might think." Then your writing purpose would be to imagine what your readers think about these animals' intelligence and to convince them to change their minds. On the other hand, your thesis might be "Whales and porpoises are so intelligent that we should show respect for these amazing creatures." Then your writing purpose would be to find the examples that would explain to your readers just how amazing these animals' intelligence is. You can see how your thesis will guide your writing. If you're wondering what to say, ask yourself, "Will this help to convince my audience that my thesis is correct?"

Some types of writing focus on your feelings. In such a case your thesis might be "Why the day I didn't get asked to the school dance was one of the worst days of my life." Your writing purpose would be to explain to your audience what was so terrible about the experience, or to help them to feel what you felt, so that they could understand why the day was so bad.

Other types of writing are supposed to focus on facts. In such a case, be sure to pick a thesis that can be supported by facts. If your teacher is expecting a factual paper and you write about "Why I think porpoises are beautiful animals," you will have missed the point of the assignment. You may have an *opinion*—for example, "We should show more respect for whales and porpoises than we do now because they are so intelligent." That opinion, however, needs to be supported by facts: how these sea animals show their intelligence; how people do not show respect for these animals.

A good thesis should be written in one sentence, and it should require some argument or explanation, so that you will either convince your audience to agree with your thesis or explain to them what they need to know to understand it. "I like rock music" is not as good a thesis as "Rock music often helps me get through hard times." The first thesis statement does not need to be explained: you like what you like. The second statement not only needs to be explained, but it also points the way for what you need to say to reach your audience. (Which hard times are you talking about? How has rock music helped?)

To help you bring your audience, your topic, your thesis, and your writing purpose together, use one of the following statements, filling in the blanks. Then copy whichever completed sentence works best for you and keep it in front of you while you are proceeding through the rest of the writing process. You may wish to change it at various points, as you come to understand your ideas and feelings better, or as your ideas change. Having a clear thesis statement and writing purpose —even one that changes—is your best guarantee of a clear and focused essay.

My Writing Purpose

I want to *convince* _____ that

(my audience)

_____ .

(my thesis sentence)

I want to *explain* to _____ that

(my audience)

_____ .

(my thesis sentence)

I want _____ to *feel* that

(my audience)

_____ .

(my thesis sentence)

Chapter 3:
Brainstorming
(Letting It All Hang Out!)

As we saw in Chapter 1, brainstorming is the technique of writing everything you know about a topic, with the purpose of freeing your thoughts. There are many different ways to brainstorm, but key to all of them is this idea: *Don't criticize yourself.* Don't stop to wonder if your ideas are good or bad, or if they are spelled correctly or put into Standard English. Brainstorming is for *you.*

When to Brainstorm

You can use this technique throughout the writing process, whenever you feel stuck for ideas or just want to loosen your mind up a little. Whenever else you use this technique, it's a good idea to brainstorm at the beginning of the writing process to get yourself started.

You can brainstorm before or after you've chosen a writing purpose and a thesis. For example, if you've been assigned an essay on "How I Spent My Summer Vacation," you may need to do a little brainstorming to come up with an audience and a thesis. You might brainstorm ideas for an audience:

Aunt Martha	someone in Mexico
José	me after I graduate high school

Writing these ideas down may help you decide to whom you are writing. That, in turn, will help you think of what you want to say. After all, you'd describe your vacation differently to Aunt Martha than you would to someone who had never been to the United States.

You can also brainstorm ideas about the topic itself, before or after you've chosen an audience. Perhaps the things you remember about last summer will help you decide what your main point is or to whom you'd like to tell them:

going mountain climbing	short of money
scared of heights	friends out of town
looking for a job	felt strong
cold because so high	beautiful view

The writer who brainstormed the ideas above spent the summer looking for work, with one trip out of town that included mountain climbing. That writer could use those brainstorming ideas to narrow the topic—to write about either looking for work or mountain climbing—and to choose a thesis: "Mountain climbing is difficult but worthwhile because once you've climbed the mountain, you feel strong," or "This was a difficult summer because my friends were out of town and I didn't have a job."

Once you've found a writing purpose—a thesis plus an audience—you might want to brainstorm further. Picture your audience. Then picture what you have to tell that audience to convince them that your thesis is true, explain your thesis to them,

28

or create interest in your thesis. As you picture different points you might make or examples you might give, write them down. That's brainstorming.

Questions That Will Help You Brainstorm

Sometimes it's hard to get yourself started on a topic. Brainstorming is supposed to help you remember what you already think and feel—but suppose you try to brainstorm and don't come up with any ideas?

Don't worry. Many writers, even people who write for a living, often feel that they have "nothing to say" when they first sit down to write. Usually these feelings come out of nervousness. In reality, the writer does have an idea but worries that the idea may not be "good enough." Writers learn various "tricks" to stop worrying long enough to find out their own ideas. You can learn them, too. As you get more practice writing, you may even find yourself coming up with some tricks of your own.

For an Opinion-Based Paper

Sometimes your writing assignments will concern your feelings, experiences, or opinions. Your teacher will not be interested so much in your using facts as in your exploring what you feel and think about a topic. Writing assignments like "My Most Unforgettable Experience," "What It Means to Me to Be a Citizen," "Why I Think the Driving Age Should Be Lowered," "My Best Friend," and, yes, "What I Did on My Summer Vacation" come under this category.

Here are some questions you can ask to get yourself going:

► How does this topic make me feel? Am I angry? Sad? Happy? Scared? Why?

► Did something happen to me or someone I know that reminds me of this topic? (For example, if you're being asked to write about what it means to be a citizen, you may know someone who became a U.S. citizen or who wants to become one. If you're writing about the driving age, you might remember a time when it would have helped you to be able to drive a car.)

► Whom do I know that doesn't feel at all the way I do about this topic? (This could be someone who has a different opinion—for example, an adult you know who doesn't think teenagers should drive. Or just someone who has a different feeling, for example, a friend who doesn't like your best friend.) What does that person think or feel about this topic? How are my thoughts and feelings different?

► How did I feel about this topic last year? Five years ago? Why do I feel differently now, or why do I feel the same now? (Maybe you never thought about the driving age when you were seven years old, but now that you are older, it might really bother you not to be able to drive. Why? What's important about driving to you that wasn't important to you when you were seven?)

► How do I imagine I will think or feel about this topic next year? After I graduate? Will this question be more important, less important, or the same? Why? (Maybe you imagine that your best friend will always be your best friend. Why? What qualities about this person make him or her someone who will stay a friend to you? What feelings do you have about this person? Why would you be glad to keep this person as a friend?)

For a Fact-Based Paper

Sometimes you have to write a research paper or a paper that depends on facts. Your teacher may not be as interested in your feelings about whales and porpoises as in what you have found out about how intelligent they are. You can still use brainstorming to get started on this type of paper.

First, since brainstorming is for you and you alone, you can still write down how you feel, even if these feelings won't be part of your final writing. A fact-based paper won't end with your feelings, but it might start with them. If you feel sad when you think of whales, for example, you can ask yourself why. If the answer is "Because I know they are in danger," that leads you to ask, "Why are they in danger?" This kind of brainstorming could lead you to write a very interesting paper on how whales are an endangered species and what people can do to save them. The paper won't be about your feelings, but your feelings will have helped you get started.

Second, the more you brainstorm about your ideas, the more ideas you are likely to have. That way, instead of feeling that you have nothing to say, you'll have the problem of choosing the best idea out of a list of several.

You can brainstorm ideas for a research paper both before and after you actually do the research. When you brainstorm before doing research, you will find it helpful to ask yourself the following questions:

31

► What do I most want to know about this topic? (**Hint:** Every answer usually leads to another question. If you feel that you're a little stuck, try thinking about where your answers lead. For example, let's say your topic is "Greek Mythology." Maybe what you most want to know about Greek mythology is how the different gods and goddesses were related to each other. That might lead you to ask the question, "Where did the Greeks think the gods came from?" or "How did the Greeks think the world was started?")

► What do I already know about this topic? (Write down anything that comes into your mind. For example, you might think that you don't know anything about Greek mythology, except that sometimes stars and constellations have Greek names. That might not seem like an important fact, but it could lead you into doing research on Greek myths about stars and constellations. Perhaps you know that myths are like stories. That could lead you to look for books that tell the stories of different myths.)

► Why is this topic important to me? What difference would it make if I didn't know anything about it? (You might have a lot of ideas that would answer this question, or you might think, "Actually, I don't see how this topic matters to me at all!" Even if that's what you think, you might find it helpful to start looking for a reason why the topic *might* be important. What possible answers could there be to that question? "Making up" or "guessing" answers might spark some ideas.)

Brainstorming ideas in this way might give you some questions that you can then use your research to answer. For example, someone brainstorming on Greek mythology might decide that what he or she was most interested in was Greek stories about the stars. Someone else could decide that he or she was interested in how the Greeks worshiped their gods. Each of these people would be looking for different books and asking different questions during his or her research.

Once you've finished your research, you might sit down and ask yourself these questions:

► What is important to me about this topic?
► What will be interesting to my audience about this topic?
► What surprised me in my research?
► What's the first thing that comes to mind now when I think of this topic?

Answering these questions can help you find a writing purpose. It can also help you to organize your material. When you see what came to your mind as "most important" or "most interesting" about your material, you can choose to spend more time writing about that.

Remember, whenever you feel "stuck," ask yourself how you feel about your topic, what seems important to you about it, or what your audience needs to know about it. You can also ask yourself what your audience needs to hear in order to feel interested in or persuaded by your thesis. Letting your mind wander a little is often the best way of getting yourself back on track.

Chapter 4:
Organizing Your Ideas
(Getting It Together)

Once you've finished your brainstorming—and your research, if you're writing a research paper— you are ready to organize your ideas. Organizing your ideas means getting them into an order that will make sense to both you and your reader. It means making an outline or some other set of notes that will guide you through your writing, so that you know which idea to cover first, next, and so on. Organizing is a very helpful step to complete before you start writing. It means that you can separate *thinking* about your ideas from *writing* them down.

Many writers find that the best form of organization is an outline. There are many ways to write an outline. You can make a very sketchy outline that is really just a list of different ideas. You can make a detailed outline that shows exactly what you are going to say about each idea, using full sentences and lots of facts and examples. You can also do anything in between. You'll discover through experience which type of outline works best for you.

The advantage of a very detailed outline is that it leaves less thinking to do while you are actually writing. You can just "follow the directions" laid out in your outline. However, some people find that they change their minds a lot while they are writing. To these people, a detailed outline is a waste of time, because they will not follow the details. You will probably also find that you need different types of outlines for different projects. A ten-page research paper on the discovery of penicillin would probably need a more detailed outline than a two-page essay about your best friend.

Preparing for Your Outline

Three steps that you can take to organize your ideas and that will get you ready to write your outline are (1) eliminate unimportant ideas, (2) group and label your ideas, and (3) choose an order for your ideas.

Eliminate Unimportant Ideas

As you look at your brainstorming or at your research, decide which ideas or facts are unimportant or don't really relate to your thesis. For example, here is an example of a writer's brainstorming for an essay on the topic "Things That Should Be Changed at Our School." The writer had already chosen a thesis and an audience, so her writing purpose looked like this:

> I want to *convince the principal of our school* that *students should be allowed to leave school during lunch hour.*

Brainstorming

not enough fresh air in cafeteria	boring study halls
choices	long lines
exercise is important	better food
vegetarians	food fights

35

The writer went over her brainstorming and decided which ideas would be useful. The other ideas she crossed out.

Brainstorming

not enough fresh air in cafeteria	~~boring study halls~~
choices	long lines
~~exercise is important~~	better food
vegetarians	food fights

The writer looked at the brainstorming again. She was pleased that she had eliminated two ideas— "boring study halls" and "exercise is important"— that did not seem to relate to her thesis. Then she decided that she would also cross out "food fights." When she had written that idea, she had thought that one reason students might want to leave school during lunch hour would be to avoid food fights in the cafeteria. However, as she thought about her writing purpose she decided that this idea would not be good to include. Her audience (the principal) would probably think that if students were irresponsible enough to have food fights, they should not be allowed to leave school! The final list looked like this:

Brainstorming

not enough fresh air in cafeteria	~~boring study halls~~
choices	long lines
~~exercise is important~~	better food
vegetarians	~~food fights~~

The writer had eliminated ideas that were not important or that did not support her writing purpose. Now she was ready for the next step in organizing her ideas.

Group and Label Your Ideas

Now that you've gotten rid of your least important ideas, you're ready to start playing with the ideas that are left. You may find that you eliminate some of these ideas, too, or that you combine one or more ideas together. Begin by organizing these ideas into groups. Label each group, so that you can be sure that each idea is where it belongs.

Here is how the writer of the lunch-hour paper grouped her ideas:

choices	not enough fresh air in cafeteria
better food	long lines
vegetarians	

Then she gave each group a label:

Reasons Why Restaurants Are Good	*Reasons Why Cafeteria Is Bad*
choices	not enough fresh air in cafeteria
better food	
vegetarians	long lines

Sometimes grouping your ideas in this way will give you more ideas. Now that the writer of the lunch-hour paper has two labels, she can think of more reasons why restaurants are good and why the cafeteria is bad. She may also want to come up with some new labels and some more ideas. Organizing her ideas lets her see what she has and what she doesn't have.

When you are organizing your ideas for a research paper, you may find that you have several pages of notes or many note cards to organize. You may wish to use different colors for each point, so that you can see at a glance how your ideas are grouped. Some people find it helpful to recopy their notes into groups if there are not too many notes. Other people like to color-code their notes and then copy them into an outline. People who use note cards often make different piles of note cards and label each pile. You can experiment until you find the method of organizing that is right for you. Just remember to *group* and *label* your ideas. Eliminate any ideas that don't seem to fit your thesis once you have grouped and labeled everything.

Choose an Order for Your Ideas

Now that you have labeled each group of ideas, you don't have to deal with every single one. You can look at just the labels and decide in which order they should be.

The writer of the lunch-hour paper looked at her two labels and decided they should go in the following order:

1. Reasons Why Cafeteria Is Bad
2. Reasons Why Restaurants Are Good

There are several different orders for ideas. Here are some of the most common:

chronological—Start with the latest information and work backward, or start with the earliest information and work forward. This order is very useful for writing history papers or describing important experiences.

compare and contrast—Go back and forth between two different arguments; or give all the reasons for one side of the story first, then all the reasons for the opposing view. This form is very useful for papers that are supposed to present more than one opinion about a question. Even if you are arguing for one opinion, you might want to present your case first, then say what people who disagree with you believe, then answer all their arguments. On the other hand, you could go through each opposing argument in turn and knock it down.

order of importance—Start with the most important idea and move down through less important ideas, until you reach the least important information. This is the way news stories are written, so that if people don't have time to read the whole article, they will at least have read the most important facts. On the other hand, you can start with the least important information and work your way up to the most important. Many opinion papers use this form of organization. The reader's interest is held because he or she wants to find out what the more important arguments are.

general to specific—Sometimes, it's effective to start out by clearly stating your thesis and your main ideas and then give examples, going from the general to the specific. For example, the writer of a paper on why we need to save the whales might begin by explaining that whales are in danger, then give examples of all the different threats that whales face. On the other hand, it's also effective to start with the specific and work your way up to the general. The writer of the whale paper might begin by describing the different dangers and then make the main point: "Whales are in danger and it's up to us to save them.'' This format often works well for research papers.

Whichever order you choose for your ideas, remember that the most important question you need to answer is ''What does my audience need to know?'' If you are writing a book report, your audience may need to read the summary of the plot before going on to read about your opinion. If you are arguing that the school should let students leave the premises during lunch hour, you may need to convince your reader that there are problems with the cafeteria before explaining how much better a restaurant would be. Whenever you are unsure of how to order your ideas, go back to your writing purpose and think about your audience.

Making an Outline

Now that your ideas are organized, you are ready to put them into an outline form. The advantage of this form is that it is quick and easy to read. It shows you at a glance what you have to write now and what you need to leave for later. It also helps you identify gaps—ideas, facts, or examples that you have to include.

An outline uses Roman numerals, letters, and Arabic numerals to show main ideas, secondary ideas, and examples. Here is the outline that the writer of the lunch-hour paper wrote. Notice how she made use of the groupings of ideas and the labels she had written. Notice also how she expanded the wording that she used in brainstorming so her outline would tell her exactly what to say:

I. Reasons Why Cafeteria Is Bad
   A. Not enough fresh air in cafeteria
   B. Cafeteria has long lines
II. Reasons Why Restaurants Are Good
   A. More choices
   B. Better food
   C. Vegetarians can find more food

This was a good start, but the outline still needed work. First, the writer decided to switch the order of "More choices" and "Better food." She thought that "More choices" and "Vegetarians can find more food" went together, because vegetarians needed special kinds of choices. Then she realized that "Vegetarians can find more food" was an *example* of "More choices." So she rewrote the outline to look like this:

II. Reasons Why Restaurants Are Good
   A. Better food
   B. More choices
      1. Vegetarians can find more food

Now she needed more examples of the various points. So she expanded her outline to look like this:

I. Reasons Why Cafeteria Is Bad
   A. Cafeteria has long lines
      1. Students might miss class
      2. Have to eat too fast
   B. Not enough fresh air in cafeteria
II. Reasons Why Restaurants Are Good
   A. Better food
   B. More choices
      1. Vegetarians can find more food
      2. People on diets

Notice that expanding the outline did not mean making every point into a full sentence. It meant adding new ideas and making sure each idea was clear. The writer also rearranged the order of the points under "I." She decided to begin with the most important idea (that the cafeteria had long lines)—and then go on to the less important idea (that the cafeteria didn't have enough fresh air).

As you can see, working on your outline can save you a lot of work later when you are actually writing your paper. The more ideas you have now, the easier you will find it to play around with the order of your ideas. It's also easier to think of new ideas when all you have to write is a word or two in an outline, instead of a whole sentence or paragraph. Look at the writer's last outline, on page 41, and compare it to her first outline. Which outline do you think would make it easier to write a paper? Can you think of other ideas and further improvements that this writer might make?

Of course, an outline is only a guide. If you find as you write that you want to use a different order or other examples from those listed in your outline, or if you want to cut out some ideas that now seem less interesting, you should go ahead and do so. Even this kind of revision is easier if you have a written outline instead of just random thoughts in your head. In fact, if you get new ideas while writing your paper, you might want to go back and revise your outline, or make a new one, before writing any further.

Chapter 5:
Writing Your First Draft
(Roughing It!)

Some people call a first draft a *rough draft* instead. Both terms make the same point: This is the first, rough version of your final paper. It isn't supposed to be perfect. It isn't supposed to be finished. It's just supposed to be your ideas down on paper, so that you will have the chance to see what they look like and decide what you want to do next.

You will find that your outline is very useful to you in writing your first draft. You can focus on each point in the outline as it comes up, without having to think of the whole paper at once. You can spend some time thinking about each point without worrying that you'll forget what your next point is supposed to be. When you're done with the point you're working on, you can just look back at the outline to remember what comes next.

However, even though you've got an outline, you may still want to do more organizing of your ideas. Most outlines suggest ideas for paragraphs, but few are detailed enough to show you how each paragraph should be organized. You may need to make mini-outlines to help organize your ideas within each paragraph.

Writing Strong Paragraphs

A paragraph is a unit within a piece of writing. It expresses a main thought and related ideas. The main thought in a paragraph is often expressed in a *topic sentence.* The topic sentence can come at the beginning, end, or middle of a paragraph. Some paragraphs don't have topic sentences: Their main thoughts are suggested, not stated explicitly. You are free to choose the style of writing that is most comfortable for you. However, if you feel that you sometimes have difficulty organizing your thoughts, you might try writing explicit topic sentences to help you structure your paragraphs.

Just like the topic for a paper, the topic for a paragraph should be neither too broad nor too narrow. A topic sentence like ''Horses are beautiful animals'' is probably too broad for a good paragraph. A sentence like ''Racehorses require careful training'' is more specific, but may still be a little too broad. ''Racehorses require careful training from the moment they are born'' is a better topic sentence. It tells you exactly what the paragraph will be about. You can see that any ideas that do not relate to this topic sentence will belong in another paragraph.

On the other hand, a topic sentence like ''Some horses run almost fifty miles per hour'' might be too narrow. To broaden that topic sentence, you might write instead, ''Racehorses run surprisingly fast, but there are some other animals that run even faster.''

The reason our two topic sentences are useful—neither too broad nor too narrow—is because they leave room for the paragraph to develop. Both sentences suggest other ideas, examples, or facts that can be used to explain the topic sentence. Both sentences are specific enough to suggest more ideas, but not so specific that there is nothing left to say.

Here are the two topic sentences, with one writer's ideas of how to develop them.

Racehorses require careful training from the moment they are born.
- ► getting used to humans
- ► learn to come for food
- ► learn saddle and bridle
- ► reins steer them

Racehorses run surprisingly fast, but there are some other animals that run even faster.
- ► racehorses run almost fifty miles per hour
- ► cheetah is fastest animal—seventy miles per hour
- ► antelope also runs faster than horse
- ► horse runs faster than most other animals, including reindeer, zebra, and humans

In the first example, the writer went on to *explain* the careful training that racehorses receive. Because the topic sentence included the words "from the moment they are born," the writer knew he had to start describing the training from that moment and continue until the training was over.

In the second example, the writer *gave examples and details.* First, he gave the detail of how fast racehorses run. Then he explained which other animals "run even faster." Then he went back to his first idea, reminding the reader that horses *do* run faster than most animals.

You can imagine how easy it would be for a writer to develop a paragraph from the topic sentences and ideas given. You might try practicing your paragraph writing by trying to write your own versions of those two paragraphs. Then compare them with this writer's versions:

From the moment that it is born, a racehorse must learn to get used to human beings. It has to be taught how to come for food as soon as it is old enough to leave its mother. When the horse gets older, it must get used to a saddle and bridle. Finally, a good racehorse must learn how to be guided by reins. *Racehorses require careful training from the moment they are born.*

A horse can run faster than most other animals, including reindeer and zebra. And of course, a horse runs faster than a human being! *However, although racehorses run surprisingly fast, there are some other animals that run even faster.* A racehorse can run almost fifty miles per hour—but a cheetah, the fastest animal on earth, can run seventy miles per hour.

Did you notice that in the first paragraph, the topic sentence came at the end, whereas in the second paragraph, it came in the middle? The topic sentence might also have come at the beginning. Once you know what the topic sentence is and which ideas will be included in the paragraph, you are free to try out different orders for the ideas. Just be sure that the order you choose makes sense and that the reader has all the necessary information.

Using Your Outline to Write Paragraphs

Go back and look at the outline for the paper on eating outside the cafeteria on page 41 of the previous chapter. The material after the capital letters in that outline might make the beginnings of good topic sentences for paragraphs. The material after the Arabic numerals below those letters might be used in some of the sentences in the paragraphs.

Depending on how detailed an outline you write, you may find that the material after the Roman numerals, capital letters, or Arabic numerals may form the basis of topic sentences for your paragraphs. In any case, a good outline will suggest many topic sentences to you. Here is the way the writer of that outline developed her first two paragraphs.

    A. Cafeteria has long lines
       1. Students might miss class
       2. Have to eat too fast
    B. Not enough fresh air in cafeteria

First Topic Sentence
One reason why students should be allowed to leave school during lunch hour is the long lines in the cafeteria.

Supporting Ideas
► Students might miss class
► Have to eat too fast
► Students should be allowed to go somewhere faster

Second Topic Sentence
The cafeteria is also an unpleasant place to many students.

Supporting Ideas
► Not enough fresh air
► Too crowded
► Too noisy

First Draft of Two Paragraphs
One reason why students should be allowed to leave school during lunch hour is the long lines in the cafeteria. Long lines mean students might miss class. They might have to eat too fast. Students should be allowed to go somewhere they can get food more quickly.

The cafeteria is usually quite stuffy. It is also crowded and noisy. *The cafeteria is an unpleasant place for many students.*

The writer can improve her writing style and tone, but she knows that this is just a first draft. What's important is whether she has put her ideas down in a form with which she can work. In that sense, this writer was very successful. She has written two paragraphs that include the ideas from her outline. Later, she can polish them.

Notice how the topic sentence in each paragraph is in a different place. The writer has used the topic sentence she wrote, and she has used the supporting ideas in the order she developed. She has varied her writing by putting one topic sentence at the beginning of a paragraph and the other one at the end.

Notice also how the writer had to change point B on her outline to make a good topic sentence. As it was written in the outline, B was far too specific to make a good topic sentence. Once you say that there is not enough fresh air in the cafeteria, what else is there to say? But saying that the cafeteria might be an unpleasant place suggested that the writer should give examples. One example of how it was unpleasant was the lack of fresh air, but the writer found other examples as well. You can see how an outline is useful, but can also be changed while you are writing. In addition, you can see why it's good to organize your ideas paragraph by paragraph.

Developing a Paragraph

Usually, a good topic sentence will suggest what else you need to say in your paragraph. Nevertheless, here are some ideas for ways to develop a paragraph from a topic sentence.

Facts. Sometimes a topic sentence simply needs to be supported with statistics or statements of fact. The paragraph about the speed of a racehorse, for example, was developed by giving the names of the animals that ran more slowly than a horse, the name of the animal that ran faster, and the speeds of the horse and the fastest animal. Facts are useful in developing paragraphs in research papers. One or two facts can also be useful in a paper that is expressing an opinion.

Reasons. The writer of the lunch-hour paper used reasons to develop her first paragraph. She complained about the long lines, then she gave reasons why she didn't like them. If you are asked to write a paper about why you are for or against something, you will find it useful to develop paragraphs with reasons.

Stories. Sometimes the best way to develop a paragraph can be with a story or an extended example. The writer of the paragraph about racehorses needing training, for example, might have developed that paragraph by telling the story of what happened to a racehorse that did not receive the proper training. Stories that are about you or people you know are useful for personal essays. Examples are useful for all types of writing.

Chapter 6:
Openers
(Catching the Reader's Attention)

The first sentence or paragraph of a piece of your writing is very important. Since it's the first thing the audience reads, it sets the mood, tells what the piece is going to be about and invites the reader to read further. In fact, the opening of an essay is so important that some writers choose to write it last!

As with every other aspect of writing, you have a lot of choices for how to open your paper. Keep in mind that a good opening should grab the reader's attention as well as set the direction of the piece. Here are some of the ways you might choose to do that.

Questions

Do you think a question is a good way to begin a piece? You can see from this example that it does get readers' attention, involving them in your writing right away. Some questions are *rhetorical*, meaning that the answer is obvious and the author is not really asking; for example:

> Would you spend money every day for a dose of poison?

Clearly, the author is not asking a real question—no one would possibly answer yes. However, the author's point becomes clear as we read on:

Would you spend money every day for a dose of poison? Well, that's exactly what you are doing when you buy a pack of cigarettes.

Questions are often a good way to begin an opinion piece, because they demand that the reader think about a question that concerns the author:

Is it fair that someone who is seventeen is allowed into any movie in town, whereas someone who is sixteen and eleven months is not?

The author might have chosen to put this question in the form of a statement:

In my opinion, it is not fair that someone who is seventeen is allowed into any movie in town, whereas someone who is sixteen and eleven months is not.

However, by putting the statement in the form of a question, the author has drawn the reader in. Readers must ask themselves whether or not they think age limits on moviegoers are fair. They have begun to be interested in the author's topic and will probably read further.

You can also use questions to begin a paragraph in the middle of your piece:

But how did the ratings system get started if it was so controversial?

Questions are a very useful way to keep a reader's interest, but be careful. Used too often, questions can become a boring device, rather than an interesting way to attract a reader's attention.

Thesis Statements

Sometimes the best way to begin a piece is by a straightforward statement of your thesis. What is the main idea that you want your audience to understand? If you can express this idea in one sentence—as you have done in your thesis—you may wish to begin your paper with it. For example:

> Whales today are facing dangers that threaten the survival of the entire species.

> What our school needs most is permission for students to leave the building during lunch hour.

> Ratings systems for movies are unfair to teenagers, who are old enough to choose their own movies.

Each of these openings is a strong, clear statement of the writer's thesis. It tells the reader exactly what the piece will be about—and it helps the writer direct the piece as well. A writer who used one of the three openings above would be able to go on and develop reasons for the opinions given, or to present facts that explain the ideas further.

Sometimes you can make use of your writing purpose in your opening. First, think of what your audience is likely to believe. Then, think of what you would like your audience to believe.

> Most people prefer the latest styles in rock music, but earlier types of music can also be very interesting.

The writer of this opening has chosen lovers of rock music as his audience. So he begins his piece by speaking directly to them: "Most people prefer the latest styles in rock music." What does this writer want his audience to believe?—that "earlier types of music can also be very interesting." This is an effective opening because it lets readers recognize themselves. If a reader is a lover of rock music, he or she may think, "Yes, that's true, most people, including me, prefer the latest styles of rock." Having already agreed with something the writer said, the reader is more ready to read the next statement.

A straightforward thesis statement is a very good way to begin an opinion paper, a research paper, or any type of fact-based writing. A two-part thesis statement, mentioning an audience plus a thesis, is an effective way to begin an opinion paper. It is also a good opening for a news article.

Stories, Jokes, and Examples

There's an old story about a frog and a centipede in which the frog asks the centipede how she knows which leg to use. Although the centipede could walk perfectly well before she met the frog, all of a sudden she began to think about which leg to use next. The first one? The fiftieth one? The ninety-fifth one? The centipede became so frantic trying to decide which leg to use that eventually she couldn't walk at all!

The writer who worries too much about what to say and how to say it may be a little like that centipede.

A story, joke, or example can be an excellent opening for a piece. As you can see, it grabs the reader's attention right away. If the story is at all interesting, the reader will want to finish it and then find out how it relates to the writer's point. If you use this type of opening, make sure that you explain clearly what the reader is supposed to learn from your story.

A personal story can be an effective way to begin an essay about a personal experience. This type of opening is also good for an opinion piece, because it hooks the reader's attention and then lets you show how the story supports your opinion. In most cases, this type of opening is not as effective for a research paper. However, many news stories begin with a story that dramatizes the article's topic:

Every Friday after school, Julie Vega gets on the bus and rides to the hospital. Julie isn't sick —she's one of the many students at Douglass School who do after-school volunteer work.

Chapter 7:
Transitions
(Getting From Here to There)

A *transition* is a way of getting from one point to the next in a paper. It shows how each idea is connected to the one that came before. Without transitions, your writing may be difficult to read. It may seem choppy and hard to follow.

One kind of transition is to repeat a word that shows your main idea, or to use a pronoun to indicate that word. Look at the first paragraph in this chapter. Can you see the transitions? Here is that same paragraph with the transitions underlined:

> A <u>transition</u> is a way of getting from one point to the next in a paper. <u>It</u> shows how each idea is connected to the one that came before. <u>Without</u> <u>transitions,</u> your <u>writing</u> may be difficult to read. <u>It</u> may seem choppy and hard to follow.

By repeating the word *transitions,* and by using *it* to refer to *transitions* and to *writing,* the writer has shown you how each idea flows into the next.

In addition to pronouns, you can use *this, that, these,* and *those* as adjectives to form transitions, as in the following paragraph:

The people I admire the most are jazz musicians. <u>These</u> remarkable men and women must not only know how to read music, but <u>they</u> must also be able to create music on the spot. <u>This</u> music is called improvisation. To me, <u>it</u> is an amazing sight to see—and hear!

In addition to pronouns and a repetition of your ideas, there are many words that show relationships between ideas. You can use these words to link your ideas within and between paragraphs.

Words That Show Examples
for example, for instance, one example of this is, in other words, say

---

A jazz musician has to be ready for anything. <u>For example</u>, <u>say</u> the pianist in a group decides to try something new one night. The bass player must be ready to change his or her performance to fit what the pianist is doing. <u>In other words</u>, anything can happen.

Try reading the above paragraph without the underlined words. The paragraph may still make sense. All the sentences are still complete sentences. However, without the transitional words, it isn't clear how each sentence relates to the ones before and after.

Words That Show Contrast
on the other hand, otherwise, nevertheless, however, but, yet, nonetheless, still, in spite of

---

On the other hand, jazz musicians cannot do anything they please. It is true that the musicians improvise, but they follow specific rules while they play, and they agree ahead of time how long each person will play. Otherwise, there would certainly be chaos! Nevertheless, a jazz musician has a freedom that a classical musician does not.

Try reading the above paragraph substituting different transitional words for the ones that are underlined. Do you see what a difference the right choice of transitional words can make? Not only do transitional words help sentences flow more smoothly, but they also show exactly what the relationship is between ideas.

When you are using transitional words that indicate contrasts, be careful. Try not to go back and forth too much within one paragraph. If you find yourself starting more than one sentence in a row with *but, however,* or *on the other hand,* you may want to reorganize your paragraph.

Words That Show Results
therefore, because, thus, consequently, so, as a result

Because of his wide range of styles, Duke Ellington is considered one of the greatest jazz composers in the world. Therefore, many other musicians have studied his musical experiments. As a result, Ellington's style can be heard not only in his own music, but also in the songs of other composers.

58

Words That Show That Another Thought
Is Being Added
and, furthermore, in addition, likewise, another, next, finally, besides, again, similarly, first of all, secondly

Jazz is one type of music that began in the United States. However, there are many different types of jazz. One jazz style began in St. Louis. <u>Another</u> came from Chicago. <u>Still another</u> began in New York. As different cities formed their own jazz styles, the music changed and grew. <u>Likewise,</u> jazz is often joined with other styles of music, such as rock or salsa, to produce new forms.

Words That Show a Relationship in Time or Space
first, second, third (etc.), meanwhile, now, then, later, eventually, soon, afterward, finally, since, nearby, beyond, in front, in back, to the right, to the left, above, below

The old musician came into the practice room. <u>First,</u> he looked at the music on the stand. <u>Then</u> he began to examine his clarinet. <u>Finally,</u> he was ready to play. The rest of the group arrived <u>soon afterward.</u>

The pianist took her place off <u>to the left.</u> <u>In front</u> of her stood the singer. The musicians got their instruments ready and began to play.

As you can see, transitions make it easy to picture how, when, and where events take place. If you think your writing might be confusing or difficult to follow, take a look at the transitions. Perhaps you have left some transitional words out or used words that did not clearly convey your meaning. Perhaps you need to repeat a key word or use a pronoun to refer to a main idea in order to remind the reader what you are talking about. You use transitions naturally when you talk, telling a story or giving directions. With a little practice, you will find it just as natural to use transitions in your writing.

Chapter 8:
Closings
(Wrapping It Up)

The way your writing ends can be almost as important as the way it begins. The closing of your paper is the last thing your reader will read. It is your chance to leave your reader with a clear idea or a strong feeling. It's your opportunity to reinforce your writing purpose by reminding your audience of your thesis.

Main Idea Closings

Usually a closing sums up or repeats a paper's main idea. When you organize your ideas into an outline, you will probably want to add one point at the end that describes the closing. You can use a transitional word to make your closing read more smoothly. For example, the writer of the lunch-hour paper wrote the following closing:

> Lunch hour is an important time for students. It is their chance to relax a little and get their strength back for the rest of the afternoon. <u>Therefore,</u> they should be able to spend their lunch hour in the most pleasant atmosphere possible. For some students, that may not be the school cafeteria.

Therefore, finally, as a result, and *so* are often useful words for closings, because they suggest summing up. You can also write *to sum up* or *in conclusion,* but be careful. Using these phrases can make your closing sound stiff and artificial.

The writer of the lunch-hour paper used her closing to repeat her main idea: Students should not have to remain in the cafeteria during lunch hour. However, in addition to repeating her main idea, she elaborated on it. She talked about students' need to relax and their need for a pleasant atmosphere. She reminded the audience both what her main idea was and why it was important.

Personal Opinion Closings

Sometimes a closing is a good time to state a personal opinion, even if you have not done so during the essay itself. In a paper on the need to save the whales, for example, a writer might spend most of the essay describing the intelligence of whales and explaining the danger these intelligent animals face. The paper could consist primarily of *facts* about whales' intelligence and danger. Then, for the closing, the writer might add something like this:

> We have just begun to learn about the special intelligence of whales. Yet these extraordinary animals face such great dangers that their whole species might be wiped out in a few years <u>if we are not careful. That is why we should all do everything we can to preserve these remarkable animals.</u>

The end of the essay is a good place for the writer's opinion in this case. If the writer has done a good job explaining why whales are remarkable and the dangers that they face, the reader will be prepared for a conclusion that tells what these facts mean to the writer.

Prediction Closings

Another type of closing gives a prediction for the future. In an essay about space travel, for example, the writer might spend most of the essay describing the history of space travel. Then the closing of the essay might look like this:

> People have been fascinated by the idea of traveling to the stars and planets ever since the beginning of human life. Now we have the ability to land on the moon. Perhaps in the future we will learn how to land on planets that are even farther away. Even if we learn to reach the limits of our solar system, people will probably always be interested in traveling farther and exploring new worlds in space.

Notice how the first part of the closing sums up the early part of the paper. The writer reminds the reader of what has already been said: that people have been fascinated by space travel for a long time, and that now we have the ability to travel at least a little way into space. Then, using the transitional phrase *Perhaps in the future,* the writer moves from what has already been said into a prediction of future events. This closing leaves the reader with a sense of how the writer's topic will continue to be important.

Closings About Feelings

Sometimes a closing reinforces a feeling or mood in the reader's mind. In a personal essay about not being able to go to a high-school dance, for example, a writer might choose the following kind of closing:

> <u>Now,</u> when I look back on that night, I know that not going to one dance did not mean that I would never have any fun again. However, <u>at the time,</u> I couldn't understand that. <u>I will always remember</u> how sad and lonely I felt in my room.

The writer wants to leave the reader with the image of being sad and lonely. Notice how the writer uses transitional words and phrases about time—*Now, at the time, I will always remember*—to make the period clear to the reader. By contrasting *now* and *at the time,* the writer leaves the reader with another perspective on the experience. By ending with *I will always remember,* the writer stresses how important the experience was—something so important that it will always be remembered.

Image and Story Closings

Finally, some closings leave the reader with a strong image or picture that reinforces the writer's point. In a news article about student volunteers, for example, a writer might end like this:

> Julie Vega works hard at her volunteer job. She says that sometimes when she gets out of school on Friday, she feels too tired to take the long bus ride to the hospital. However, when she gets there, the smiles on the faces

of the children she reads to make the long trip worthwhile. "I wouldn't give up my volunteer job for anything," Julie says. "I look forward to it all week."

Ending with the image of Julie Vega reading to the grateful children at the hospital and looking forward to her work there reinforces the writer's main idea: Volunteer work is a useful and rewarding activity. The writer could have ended by repeating that idea:

Julie Vega's work is very important both to her and to the children with whom she works. This shows how important volunteer work is and how rewarding it is to the volunteers.

Which closing do you think is more interesting? By ending with a story, the writer lets readers come to their own conclusions about why volunteer work is important. The writer chooses the story or image that seems most likely to prove the main idea, but lets readers figure the main idea out for themselves.

Closings can be difficult to write because it's often hard to choose among the different styles of closing. To choose the closing that is right for your essay, go back to your writing purpose. Who is your audience? What feeling or idea do you want your audience to have in mind? Then ask yourself which type of closing is most likely to get your audience to think or feel the way you want them to. With practice, you will enjoy writing effective conclusions to your essays and papers.

Chapter 9:
Revisions
(Taking Another Look)

You've written your first draft, gone over your opening, and added a strong, effective closing. Now it's time for the next step of the writing process: *revision*.

Revision is the stage in which you have the chance to go over your writing to make sure that you have said everything you wanted to say. It's your time to take another look and add any ideas that have come to you after finishing your first draft. It's a chance to make sure that you've said just what you meant and not accidentally ended up saying something you didn't mean. It's an opportunity to cut out ideas that don't seem to fit—or even to change your mind about what your main idea is.

To revise literally means "to see again." Now that you can see your first draft, you have the chance to look at it again. How does it look to you?

Some writers find that they are very happy during this stage. Now that the hard work of brainstorming, outlining, and writing a first draft is done, they enjoy playing with their first draft, revising it into a polished essay.

Other writers don't like this stage as much. They look at their first drafts, and instead of being pleased at the work they have already done, they are upset about the work to come. They see that their first drafts are not perfect, which they were never meant to be. This type of writer becomes discouraged at the sight of an imperfect first draft and feels even more strongly that he or she has ''nothing to say'' or ''cannot write.''

If you are the first type of writer, enjoy yourself! You've earned it. This chapter will give you some suggestions on how to revise your work, but you will be able to do so in a relaxed way because you know that almost every piece of writing needs to be revised.

If you are the second type of writer, try not to worry. The more you write, the more you will learn about how you feel at different stages of the process. If the revision stage is an uncomfortable one for you, at least you can learn to tell the difference between feeling discouraged and really believing that your writing is terrible. With practice, you will learn that no matter how discouraged you feel at this stage, you *can* revise your work successfully. Eventually, you will stop feeling discouraged and learn to have faith in yourself.

Remembering Your Writing Purpose

After you have finished your first draft, the best thing you can do is put your work away for a while. If you can leave it for a day or so, you will be surprised at how much more clearly you can see the good and the bad in your work when you come back to it. If you don't have time to leave it this long, try at least to take a half-hour break. Give yourself a treat—you've earned it! It will help you to come back to your writing in a better mood, ready to look clearly at the work that still needs to be done.

When you do come back to your work, remind yourself of your writing purpose. Who is the audience you are trying to reach? Are you trying to convince your audience, explain something, or make your audience feel a certain way? What is the thesis statement that you are trying to convey to your audience?

With your writing purpose firmly in mind, reread what you have written. If possible, read it aloud, trying to picture your audience sitting across from you, listening. Can you imagine what your audience is thinking or feeling? Is there an idea that won't be clear to this audience? Is there a sentence that seems out of place? Will this audience like the way you are presenting your argument, or will your readers be angry or offended at your "tone of voice"? Try to be as objective as possible. Jot down any ideas that come to you as you read, or make marks on your first draft—but don't stop for too long. Try to continue reading without stopping until you have come to the end.

Then, again jot down or mark any ideas that come to you. You might even brainstorm a little about what you'd like to add to, subtract from, or change in your paper. Look at your opening. Will it interest your readers? Will it tell them what your main idea is or what your writing is going to be about? Check your closing. Does it leave your readers with a strong feeling or a clear idea? Have you repeated your main idea so that it will be clear in your readers' minds?

How about your transitions? Is it clear how each sentence relates to the ones around it? Can the reader follow your ideas from paragraph to paragraph?

Checking Your Tone

Let's say you and another person are watching television together. You are hungry and want something to eat from the kitchen. What would you say to get what you want?

What you would say or do would depend on who your audience was. If you were watching television with your younger brother or sister, you might say, ''Hey! Go into the kitchen and get me some popcorn.'' If you were with a parent, you might say, ''Can I have some popcorn?'' If you were watching at a friend's house, you might ask your friend's parent, ''May I have some popcorn, please?'' The words, style, and tone of voice would be different for different audiences.

In the same way, you want the tone of your paper to fit the audience and writing purpose you have chosen. If you are writing a personal essay about something that happened to you, you might use more casual language that fits the way you would talk about the experience. If you are writing an opinion paper that is supposed to change the mind of your school principal, you might have to use more formal language. A funny essay might have lots of jokes; a serious essay might use more serious stories.

Whatever tone you use, be sure that you are comfortable with it. After all, you want your writing to sound like *you*. However, just as there are many different *you*'s—the *you* you are with your kid brother, the *you* you are with your parents, the *you* you are with strangers—so can you have many different tones and styles in your writing.

Picking a Title

Revising your work may involve writing one or more drafts after the first one, or you may simply cross out some words and add others. The choice is up to you—and will probably change depending on how long the writing assignment is and what it's about. In any case, sooner or later, you should think about writing a *title* for your piece.

Some writers like to start with a good title. Others wait until after their first draft is done. Still other writers wait until their writing has been revised before they pick a title. Whenever you do it, picking a title is important. It's another way of making your main idea clear. It also helps set the tone and attract your reader's interest.

When you look through a magazine, what is one of the things you notice first? It's probably the titles of the articles. The title can tell you whether the article will be funny or serious. It can also tell you whether the article is about something that interests you. It might even tell you the author's opinion about the subject.

Here are three different titles on the lunch-hour paper. What does each one suggest to you?

Leaving School During Lunch Hour:
Every Student's Right

Students and Their Lunch Hours

Around the Block at Twelve O'Clock

The first title states the author's topic—students leaving school during lunch hour—as well as giving the author's opinion—that students should be allowed to leave. The second title is more neutral. It tells you that the paper will be about students and lunch hours, but does not tell you what the author thinks. The third title is more humorous. It uses a rhyme and somewhat casual language for a cheerful, lighthearted tone. Each title suggests a different type of paper. The writer has to choose a title that fits the tone and purpose of his or her paper.

Sometimes it's good to use a title plus a *subtitle*. For ''Around the Block at Twelve O'Clock,'' for example, the writer might add a second title, or subtitle.

Around the Block at Twelve O'Clock:
Students Want to Leave During Lunch Hour

The subtitle adds the information necessary to explain the title.

If you are not sure what kind of title to use, you might do what news writers do. They usually write a short sentence that describes the actions or feelings of the main people, animals, places, or things in the article. Here are some ''news-style'' titles for some of the papers you've been reading so far:

Whales Face Greater Danger Than Ever
Jazz Musicians Improvise Throughout the Years
Racehorses Require Special Training for Many Years
Space Travel:
Important to People Since the Beginning

Chapter 10:
Editing Your Paper
(Becoming A Grammar Examiner)

Once you have gotten your ideas in order, looked at your tone, and come up with a title, you are ready to edit your paper. At this stage, you may still notice things about your ideas that you wish to change, but your main focus should be on checking your writing for grammar and writing style. If you find that you are still spending time on changing your ideas and tone, you may wish to do another draft.

Sooner or later, when you have accepted the ideas in your paper, it will be time for you to look at the mechanics of grammar and style. Here are some common mistakes to watch out for. Once you spot them, they're easy to correct. That's why it's a good idea to spend some time looking just for this kind of mistake, *after* you are satisfied with the rest of your paper.

Common Mistakes in Usage

Subject-Verb Agreement
Remember that every subject must agree with its verb. Remember also that some subjects are tricky. Collective nouns—like *army, herd, group,* and *class*—usually take singular verbs even though they refer to many people, animals, or things. Some nouns that

sound plural—like *ham and eggs* or *twenty dollars*—refer to only one dish or amount, and so also take singular verbs.

Remember to check the rules for compound subjects that include the word *or*. Sometimes these subjects take a plural verb and sometimes a singular one. Be sure you've made your choice correctly.

Finally, don't forget to look hard at indefinite pronouns. Remember that some indefinite pronouns are singular—like *each*, *every*, and *anyone;* some are plural—like *all* and *both;* and some can be either singular or plural, depending on how they are used. *Most*, *some*, and *a lot* come into that category.

If you have any questions about subject-verb agreement or about any other aspect of usage, check your grammar textbook or another reference book. You can also ask your teacher. Everyone has trouble sometimes remembering the correct rule. It's better to ask than to guess incorrectly.

Consistency in Verb Tenses

In most cases, a sentence that begins in one verb tense should end in that tense. It is also usually best to use the same tense throughout a paragraph, perhaps even throughout your paper.

Notice how confusing the changes in verb tense make the following paragraph from a book report:

> The book begins when Jane threw a book at her stepbrother. Then Jane goes to school. After she left school, she becomes a governess. That is when she met Mr. Rochester.

The paragraph would read better if it were all in the same tense. Usually the descriptions of book plots are written in the present tense, as though they were still happening:

> The book begins when Jane throws a book at her stepbrother. Then Jane goes to school. After she leaves school, she becomes a governess. That is when she meets Mr. Rochester.

Of course, sometimes it's necessary to change tenses in order to show a change in time. However, if you notice more than one tense in one sentence or paragraph, try making all the tenses the same. If your writing still makes sense, you might find that it also reads better when the tenses are kept consistent. You might also check to see that all the paragraphs stay in the same tense throughout your report. Make sure that if you do change tenses, you have a very good reason for it.

Pronoun-Antecedent Agreement

Remember that a pronoun and its antecedent must agree in number, person, and gender. Can you spot the lack of agreement in the following sentences?

> Readers will enjoy this adventure story. You will be on the edge of your seat all the way through!

> Almost everyone has had a time when they questioned their beliefs.

Here are the edited versions of those sentences, with the pronouns and their antecedents agreeing:

> Readers will enjoy this adventure story. They will be on the edges of their seats all the way through!

74

or: <u>You</u> will enjoy this adventure story. <u>You</u> will be on the edge of <u>your</u> seat all the way through!

Almost <u>everyone</u> has had a time when <u>he</u> <u>or she</u> questioned <u>his or her</u> beliefs.

or: <u>Most people</u> have had times when <u>they</u> questioned <u>their</u> beliefs.

Remember, it used to be considered acceptable to use *he* to stand for *everyone.* These days, however, most writers and editors agree that this usage leaves out women and girls. Generally, it's better to say *his or her.* If this is awkward (as in the first edited version of the sentence above), you can put the sentence into the plural and use *their.* Whichever choice you make, remember that most people don't consider it correct to use *their* when *everyone* is the antecedent.

Common Mistakes in Sentence Structure

Avoid Sentence Fragments

A sentence fragment is only a fragment, or part, of a sentence. It may make sense to you when you write it, but it probably won't make sense to a reader. That's why it's a good idea not to use sentence fragments. Be sure that every sentence you write has a subject and a verb and expresses a complete thought.

You can usually recognize a fragment because it forces you to ask a question about the meaning of a sentence:

Because it forces you to ask a question.

75

This fragment is very confusing. *What* forces you to ask a question? Where does the *because* come from? You need the full sentence for the thought to make sense.

Remember, the goal of clear writing is to keep the reader from having to work hard to understand you. You want all of your reader's energy to be on following your argument or feeling the emotions you are describing.

Avoid Run-On and Overly Long Sentences

Run-on sentences are hard to understand, they give the reader more than one complete thought to think about.

Do you recognize what is wrong with that sentence? A run-on combines two or more sentences into one, with a misplaced comma or no punctuation at all. It can usually be corrected with a period, a semicolon, or a comma and a conjunction (for example, *and* or *but*).

Overly long sentences are also difficult for a reader to understand because they go on and on and it's hard to tell when you can take a break and it also isn't clear what the sentence is about because there are so many ideas in it that you don't really have the energy to follow it and besides you'd probably get lost and maybe even get tired and give up before reaching the end....

Have you had enough? Most long sentences aren't as long as that one, but they have much the same effect. They keep the reader from clearly following the writer's ideas. Here is that same sentence edited down into manageable sentences:

Overly long sentences are also difficult for a reader to understand. Because they go on and on, it's hard to tell when you can take a break. It also isn't clear what the sentence is about. There are so many ideas in it that you don't really have the energy to follow it. You might even get lost or tired and give up before reaching the end.

Notice the different ways of combining phrases and clauses to make sentences of different shapes. Some sentences start with dependent clauses *(Because they go on and on)*. The writer has used some transitional words that make connections clear—*because, also, that.* The writer has also edited out some of the connecting words in the first paragraph *(besides, and)*. Be careful with connecting words. A few of them used in the right places can tie your ideas together, but too many of them used too often can make your writing sound stiff and artificial.

Avoid Dangling and Misplaced Phrases

Can you see the problems in the following sentences?

Walking down the street, a thick fog descended.

Janey returned the hat to the store that was too small.

In the first sentence, it sounds as though the fog is walking down the street! The phrase *walking down the street* is "dangling," just hanging on the end of the sentence without relating to another word. See how much less confusing the edited versions are:

As I was walking down the street, a thick fog descended.

Walking down the street, I watched the thick fog descend.

Both edited sentences make it clear *who* was walking down the street. Now the phrase *walking down the street* does not dangle, but relates to the person *I*.

In the second sentence, it sounds as though Janey went back to a small *store.* If the writer meant to say that Janey returned a small *hat,* he or she has misplaced the phrase. The edited version of the sentence is clearer:

Janey returned the hat that was too small to the store.

Everyone misplaces a phrase now and then. Take the time when you are editing your writing to make sure that you have put all phrases into their proper places. Sometimes it's necessary to rewrite a sentence to avoid the awkward placement of a long phrase or two:

Unedited: Janet returned the hat with the blue flowers to the store that was too small.

Better, But Still Awkward: Janey returned the hat with the blue flowers that was too small to the store.

Best: Janey returned to the store the hat with the blue flowers that was too small.

Pointers for Better Writing

The suggestions in this section will help make your writing clearer, more interesting, and easier to read. After you have finished revising your work and editing for grammar and sentence structure, take another look to ask yourself if you have made your writing as smooth as possible. Here are some helpful things to keep in mind.

Parallel Structure in Sentences

To use *parallel structure* means to make the different parts of your sentences match. Take a look at the following sentences:

> After school I like going out for pizza or to take a walk.

> After school I like going out for pizza or taking a walk.

> After school I like to go out for pizza or to take a walk.

Do you see how much more smoothly the second and third sentences read? That is because they use parallel structure. The *going* and *taking* match in the second sentence, just as *to go* and *to take* match in the third sentence.

Parallel structure is also important in descriptions.

> **Not Parallel:** Verna is not only a kind person, but also talented.

> **Parallel:** Verna is not only <u>kind</u>, but also <u>talented.</u>

> **Parallel:** Verna is not only <u>a kind person,</u> but also <u>a talented one.</u>

Be sure to use parallel structure when you are making comparisons as well.

> Seeing a movie is more fun than to go to a dance.

This sentence compares *seeing* to *to go to.* Here is the

same sentence edited into parallel structure:

> Seeing a movie is more fun than going to a dance.

> To see a movie is more fun than to go to a dance.

Be especially careful with parallel structure when you are using the words either...or or neither...nor.

> **Not Parallel:** Neither cheating nor to play rough will pay off in the end.

> **Parallel:** Neither to cheat nor to play rough will pay off in the end.

> **Parallel:** Neither cheating nor playing rough will pay off in the end.

Likewise, be sure to place the words *either, neither,* and *not only* right before the words they are connecting.

> **Incorrect:** Our goalie either is tired or sick.
> **Correct:** Our goalie is either tired or sick.
> **Incorrect:** She usually not only is a wonderful goalie but also a great team player.
> **Correct:** She is usually not only a wonderful goalie but also a great team player.

In the first pair of sentences, *either...or* connects the words *tired* and *sick,* so *either* must go right before the word *tired.* In the second pair of sentences, *not only...but also* connects the words *a wonderful goalie* and *a great team player,* so *not only* must go right before *a wonderful goalie.*

Sometimes you have to rewrite a sentence creatively in order to maintain parallel construction.

> **Not Parallel:** She is not only a wonderful goalie but also full of team spirit.

Parallel: She is not only <u>a wonderful goalie</u> but also <u>a great team player</u>.

The more the parts of your sentences match, the more smoothly your sentences will read.

Using Precise and Vivid Language

Which sentence gives you a better picture?

The child picked up the dog.

The tearful little boy picked up the shivering puppy.

The second sentence not only helps you to picture what happened, but also stirs up your emotions. You can react much more to the picture of a tearful little boy and a shivering puppy than to the words *child* and *dog*. The picture was made clearer and more emotional in two ways. First, the general words *child* and *dog* were replaced by more precise words, *boy* and *puppy*. Second, the writer added adjectives—*tearful, little,* and *shivering*.

The author rewrote the sentence above by using more precise nouns and adding vivid adjectives. It's also possible to use more precise verbs and vivid adverbs:

The child picked up the dog.

The child <u>snatched</u> the dog and <u>held</u> it <u>close</u>.

Again, the first sentence is neutral. The second sentence gives you a clear picture of what is happening and leaves you room to react to it emotionally.

When you are editing your writing, ask yourself whether you have described something so clearly that the reader could not imagine it any differently from what you intended.

If you write: The child picked up the dog.

Will the reader imagine this? The tearful boy snatched the puppy and held it close.

or will the reader imagine this? The frightened boy timidly lifted the poodle, holding it at arm's length.

Each sentence gives a different image and suggests different feelings that the reader might have. Ask yourself what you want the reader to see and how you want the reader to feel. Then ask yourself if you have used language that will convey your meaning, or if there is room for other pictures and feelings than the ones you mean. Look at nouns and verbs, and ask yourself if you have used vague or specific words. Could you give more detail—such as *held it close* or *holding it at arm's length*—that tells *how* something was done? Would an adjective or adverb—like *tearful* or *timidly*—make your picture clearer?

Precise and vivid language is also important when you are writing about opinions, facts, and ideas. Compare these sentences. Which tells you more about what the problem is and how the author wants you to feel about it? Which words tip you off?

> Douglass High faces a shortage of volunteers in its after-school program.
>
> Douglass High is threatened by a severe shortage of volunteers in its valuable after-school program.

The second sentence uses a more precise verb. Instead of *facing* a shortage, Douglass High *is threatened* by one. The word *threatened* immediately tips you off that the author thinks this is a serious problem and wants you to feel frightened and concerned about it. By adding the adjectives *severe* and *valuable*, the writer is further pushing you to share his or her concern. Which is worse, a shortage or a *severe* shortage? Which program would you care more about saving, an after-school program or a *valuable* after-school program?

When you edit your opinion or fact-based writing, look to see if you have used precise and vivid language to reach your audience and achieve your writing purpose. Sometimes changing just one or two words can make a whole sentence sound different.

> The students charged with cheating were suspended from school.

> The students *unfairly* charged with cheating were suspended from school.

> The students charged with cheating were *quickly* suspended from school.

> *Fortunately*, the students charged with cheating were suspended from school.

Each sentence gives you a slightly different picture of what happened and how the writer feels about it. With practice, you can learn to use precise and vivid language to control the picture you give your audience.

Varying Your Sentence Structure

Sentences can be written in many different patterns. They can be long or short, complicated or simple, or questions or statements. Writing can be made more interesting by featuring *varied* types of sentences. Compare the two paragraphs below.

83

Television shows have gotten more interesting. They used to be all about the same topic. Each show would be about a family living in the suburbs. Television shows never dealt with real problems. The most serious problem might be whether the teenage son could get a date for the big dance. There are now some shows on television that are more interesting.

Have television shows gotten more interesting? Compare today's shows to those old programs that always dealt with the same old topic: a family living in the suburbs. Television shows never dealt with real problems. Whether the teenage son could get a date for the big dance was likely to be the most serious problem you saw. Luckily, some more interesting shows are now on the air.

The two paragraphs cover exactly the same information, but the sentences in the first paragraph are very repetitive in structure. Each starts with a subject followed immediately by a verb, except for the last sentence, which begins with a somewhat flat *There are.* Each sentence is about the same length. Each sentence is a simple, declarative sentence with no extra clauses or phrases to break up the monotony.

The second paragraph begins with a question. Then it uses a command—*Compare today's shows....* Some of the sentences are long, and some are short. The second sentence is a complex sentence and uses a colon to break up the rhythm still more. Some of the sentences start with words other than the subject of the sentence. Because it has more variety, the second paragraph is more interesting to read.

Variety in sentence structure does not mean that all sentences have to be long and complicated. Sometimes a short sentence can be more effective.

> Have television shows gotten more interesting? Stop and think. Thirty years ago, television was very different from what it is today.

That *Stop and think* really breaks up the rhythm of the paragraph. The shortness of the sentence makes the reader stop. The change in rhythm also helps hold the reader's interest.

Think of varied sentence structure as being like the rhythm in a piece of music. There may be an underlying regular beat, but if all you hear is the same rhythm repeated in the melody over and over, a song will start to sound like a nursery rhyme. Songs change their rhythms to hold the listener's interest. It's the same in writing. Try reading your work aloud to get a sense of its rhythm. If you feel that every sentence is starting to sound alike, you might want to change some sentences to questions, commands, or more complicated sentence forms—or throw in a few very short sentences. As you get used to editing your work, you'll develop a feel for the rhythm of your writing.

Chapter 11:
Proofreading
(Looking at Letters and Punctuation)

Now that the writing and thinking part of your work is done, you have only one task left to do: *proofreading.* To proofread your paper is to look at it only for mistakes in spelling, capitalization, and punctuation. You are not concerned with word choice, sentence structure, or grammar anymore. Of course, if you see any easy change to make, go ahead; but try not to think about the content of your writing. Proofreading goes best if you are looking only at the letters and punctuation marks.

Checking for Spelling

One good way to check your work for spelling is to read it aloud—and backward. That's right, start with the last word of your paper and go on to the next-to-last, and so on. That way, you won't be able to pay attention to what the words mean—only to how they are spelled.

Checking for Punctuation and Capitalization

If you feel confident about this area of grammar, simply review and proofread your work. If you are unsure of the rules for punctuating or capitalizing, you might want to glance through a grammar book to remind yourself of what to look for before you start proofreading.

Remember that every sentence begins with a capital letter and ends with some form of end punctuation: a period, question mark, or exclamation point. Also remember that periods and commas always go *inside* quotation marks. Book titles should always be underlined; article and short-story titles should be in quotation marks.

Check Your Teacher's Rules

Go back to the checklist on page 16 of this book and review your teacher's requirements for the format of your assignment. Make sure that when you recopy your final draft, you are following the rules set by your teacher. Otherwise, it's possible that all your hard work will be marked down. Remember that whatever audience you chose for your reading purpose, your teacher also has to read your work. He or she will have twenty or thirty other papers to read as well, so give both of you a break and write or type neatly!

Chapter 12:
Creative Writing
(Setting Yourself Free)

Most of this book has focused on writing essays and school papers. These assignments are usually about your thoughts and feelings on a particular topic, or a summary of your research. Sometimes, however, for either yourself or an assignment, you will practice what is called *creative writing:* stories, poems, or journal writing.

Some people find creative writing much easier than other types of writing; other people find it harder. The main difference between creative and other types of writing is that when you are writing a story or poem, you are making everything up yourself. Other types of writing may involve facts. In creative writing, you may use facts—but you are also free to make facts up. You can set your story or poem in the "real world" where certain rules apply. You can also set it in a fantasy world where you decide that children are older than their parents, rain falls up instead of down, or interplanetary space travelers hop from galaxy to galaxy in their own special space modules. Some very interesting writing takes a real-world situation, such as your school, and imagines what would happen if something "out of this world" happened, such as a visit by a creature from another planet or the discovery of a magic book by one of the school's students.

If stories give you a chance to make up realistic or fantastic events, poetry gives you a chance to explore your feelings and observations. Some poems are about incidents and events, but the writer is free to focus on certain significant details or images that may "tell the story" of those events better than a long description would. Some poems are about one object or insight that means a lot to the writer.

If you are interested in writing stories and poems, the best thing to do is to read a lot. That helps you see how wide your choices are and how free you are to write whatever is important to you.

Journal writing can be anything you want it to be. Some teachers give journal assignments that have to be turned in, but many people keep private journals or diaries to record their thoughts and feelings. Since journal writing is usually not meant to be looked at by anybody else, you know that you are *really* free to make your own rules!

Just as everyone can write, everyone can write stories, poetry, and journals. Think back to when you were a little child. Didn't you pretend that your toys were alive? Did you ever make up games, dress up on Halloween, or imagine that you were friends with someone you had seen on television or read about in a book? And now, do you ever find yourself imagining what it would be like to run into a special person somewhere when the two of you are alone? All of these are ways of writing little "stories," imagining what you would say or do *if*.... Expressing these thoughts, feelings, and imaginings is what people do when they write creatively.

If you would like to try writing stories, poetry, or a journal—or if you've been given an assignment and you *have* to try out one of these forms—here are some ideas that might get you started. Remember, you may have to go through the same process we talked about in the Introduction, getting rid of your critic, Dudley Doolittle. Sometimes Dudley can be even louder when it comes to creative writing than for other types of writing. Just remind yourself that you *can* write and that what you have to say is interesting and important because *you* are saying it. Find an audience that you can picture to help encourage you, and think of a writing purpose that will tell you how to reach that audience. Even if you promise yourself that you will never show your work to anyone, which is often a good way to keep Dudley quiet, you will find it helpful to picture someone—maybe someone just like you—who needs to hear what you have to say.

Ideas for Stories

► Think of an incident that happened to you that you had strong feelings about. Imagine another character than you. Give this other person a name and a physical description so that you can really picture him or her. Then imagine what would have happened if that person had been in the incident instead of you.

► Imagine a world that seems almost perfect. It could be another planet, another country, another time in history or in the future, or even your own world with a lot of changes that you have made. Then find one thing about this world that is not perfect and that is, in fact, a big problem. Think of a main character. It could be you or someone you would like to be. What's important is that this person appears clearly in your mind. Now imagine how this person will react to the problem. Will he or she be able to change it? Will other people help, or will they be too frightened or not understand?

▶ Think of a person you know. It could be someone you know well or someone you have just seen on the street. Imagine this person in a situation in which you have *not* seen him or her. For example, if you are thinking of your best friend, imagine her on that trip to the mountains that she took last summer. If you are thinking of the man who runs the pizza stand, imagine him at home with his family. Start to picture what this person says or does, what is important to him or her, and what problems he or she must solve. Then write a story about how this person faces a problem or achieves a goal.

Ideas for Poems

▶ Think of a person who is important to you. Think of an animal, object, or place—real or imaginary—that is like this person. Describe the animal, object, or place in your poem. You can either make a direct comparison or just suggest how this animal, object, or place is like this person you are thinking of.

▶ Remember a time that was important to you, either because it was very difficult or because it was very happy. Describe this time in your poem. You can describe it directly or by comparing it to an animal, object, place, or person. You can also describe it by telling how you felt.

► Think of a problem that you would like to solve, either in your private life or in the world. Write a poem telling how this problem makes you feel and what you would like to do about it.

Ideas for Journal Writing

► Describe the day you have just spent. However, don't just say what you did. Tell how you felt about it, or what it makes you think of. If you find yourself wandering off into a description of other thoughts and feelings, or into another incident that you are reminded of, let yourself wander.

► Think back to an incident that was important to you because it made you very happy, very angry, very sad, or very frightened. Try to describe exactly what happened. Use as many specific images as possible—the color of the shirt that you wore, the smell of the room or the outdoors, the sounds that you heard during this incident. Think of your five senses—sight, hearing, touch, smell, taste—and try to write what each sense was doing.

► Think of a person who is important to you. Write as much as you can about this person. You can try to imagine how this person feels and thinks. You can describe how you have felt and thought about this person and whether your feelings have changed. Or you can tell stories about what this person has done or think of this person in an imaginary situation. Your goal is to describe the person in the way that seems most true to you.

Chapter 13:
News Writing
(Presenting the Facts)

Many of the ideas in this book can be applied to news writing. However, a few rules are slightly different, and you should keep them in mind as you write articles for newspapers and magazines.

The main rule about news writing is to *start with the most important idea*. The assumption is that the reader may not read more than the first sentence, the first paragraph, or the first page of a story. The longer the story is, the greater the chance is that the reader will not finish it. Therefore, the most important information must come first, the second most important information must come next, and so on. This is called inverted pyramid style.

How can you tell which information is the most important? This question has different answers for different types of stories. In a news story about a new school rule, for example, the most important information might be the content of the rule, or it might be the rule's wide impact. Here are two possible *leads*, or opening sentences, of a story about a change in school rules.

> Principal Jefferson announced last week that starting next month, students will be

allowed to leave the school during lunch hour if they have a note from their parents or guardians.

Hundreds of students are planning to leave the school during lunch hour at least once a week now that Principal Jefferson has announced the new school rule.

Either of these sentences would make an acceptable lead, but each serves a slightly different purpose. The focus of the first sentence is on what the new rule is. The writer has given all the essential information: when the new rule starts, what it will allow, and what students must do to take advantage of it. This would be a good lead for an article that was informing students about the rule. Even if a reader read no further than this sentence, he or she would have the basic information.

However, what if most students have already heard about the rule? In that case, the second lead might be better. This lead does not give much information about the rule itself, but it does tell you that hundreds of students will be affected by it. A reader who already knew about the rule would be interested to know how students were reacting to it—and this lead would give that information.

News stories tend to be very straightforward. They often are written in a style that uses shorter and simpler sentences than other types of writing. Many people believe that a writer's opinion should be kept out of a news story, although other people disagree. These other people argue that since every writer has an opinion anyway, that opinion belongs in the story. That way, a reader knows what the writer's opinion is instead of having to guess. You can decide for yourself whether you think news stories should be written "objectively" (as though the writer did not have an opinion on the topic) or "subjectively" (making the writer's opinion part of the story). You should also find out what the editor or teacher responsible for your school paper or magazine believes.

News stories also differ from other types of writing in that they tend to have very strict requirements for length because a newspaper or magazine usually has a limited amount of space available. That is another reason why news stories start with the most important information first. If there is not enough room in a publication, the editor may just cut some paragraphs off the end. A story has to be written so that it would still make sense even with these cuts.

Sometimes two different terms are used for newspaper and magazine writing: *news stories* and *feature stories*. A news story is about a piece of news that happened recently. A feature story is about a person, situation, or program. It is usually not tied to a specific time. For example, a news story might describe the new rule that Principal Jefferson instituted. A feature story would describe the different plans some of the students had made for lunch hour out of school. Feature stories are often longer than news stories, and sometimes there is more leeway about the writer including his or her opinion. A feature story might also be unrelated to a specific event. For example, a story about the high school's volunteer program would probably be considered a feature story.

Index